COMPLETE BLEU DE GASCOGNE TRAINING BOOK

Understand From The Origin, Finding, Personality, Socialization, Breeding, Care, Nutrition, Exercise, Health, Grooming, Love And Others Inclusive

GEORGE LINDA

1

Table of Contents

CHAPTER ONE

Basset Bleu De Gascogne

Rare dog called the Basset Bleu De Gascogne was born in France. This dog resembles a Basset Hound in appearance but has entirely distinct coloring.

They are an ancient breed, and it's possible that they were created in the Middle Ages. Even though they have a lengthy lifespan, this breed was on the verge of extinction in the 19th century. They were just just spared, and they are still fairly uncommon today.

It is uncommon to encounter this dog outside of its native France.

Some of them are in the UK, most likely as a result of the close proximity of the two nations.

They must typically be imported because they are nearly unheard of in the United States. They aren't a breed that the American Kennel Club recognizes (AKC).

The most distinctive feature of this dog is its nearly finished ticked body. They have tiny black dots on white backgrounds.

They resemble ice cream with cookies and cream on top. Aside from this, they seem and behave like a conventional hound.

Highlights

The Basset Bleu de Gascogne is an exceedingly friendly hound that gets along well with other dogs and kids. It is a highly active dog that needs frequent walks.

• This breed loves to "sing," thus they may not be suited for smaller living areas.

However, due of their hunting tendencies, they can't be trusted with smaller animals.

Facts You May Not Know About The Basset Bleu De Gascogne

1. The majority of Basset Bleu De Gascogne dogs work.

In France, this breed is frequently displayed, but they are also frequently used as working dogs. Due of their rarity, the majority of their owners are also hunters who utilize the dogs in the field.

With litters of puppies typically going to other hunters or family members, they are frequently retained within the family.

As a result of their ears frequently becoming tangled in thorns and branches, they are permitted to exhibit scars in the show ring.

2. This breed almost vanished.

The popularity of hunting drastically declined in the 19th century. The Basset Bleu De Gascogne also saw a drop in popularity due to its widespread employment as hunting dogs, almost reaching extinction. Alain Bourbon nearly single-handedly saved them. But even now, they are still relatively uncommon.

3. The AKC does not recognize them.

This breed is not at all recognized by the American Kennel Club. This is due to the fact that no owner of the breed has made the effort to register the breed, perhaps since the majority of owners reside in France.

Continue reading for a thorough description of the Basset Bleu de Gascogne's traits.

CHAPTER TWO

History

France's Gascogne area is where the Basset Bleu de Gascogne first appeared. Literally, their name means "low, blue, from Gascogny." They are mentioned in documents from the 12th century.

The Basset Bleu de Gascogne was bred to pursue hunters on foot, unlike other hounds, which were developed to follow hunters as they rode on horses. Most of their owners were French people from lower socioeconomic classes who could not buy horses.

This dog gained popularity after the revolution since peasants were not allowed to hunt before.

At the start of the 20th century, the Basset Bleu de Gascogne was indeed thought to be mostly extinct. The dog was reintroduced to the public through breeding thanks to a guy by the name of Monsieur Alain Bourbon, a breed enthusiast. Currently, France has a sizable population of this breed, but not many exist abrod.

Men And Women

A Basset Bleu De Gascogne can be either male or female with little to no difference. Males may be somewhat larger, but often not by much.

Do Pets Of This Breed Get Along Well?

This breed gets along very nicely with other dogs of all breeds. Since they like both playing and lounging around all day, you may match them with almost any other breed.

Larger dogs leaping on their backs should be your sole worry because this might result in damage.

Cats and other such pets are manageable for them. They do, however, possess strong hunting instincts, which may lead them to pursue cats. In this situation, early socialization might be beneficial, especially if you can identify self-assured cats who aren't interested in eluding a dog.

CHAPTER THREE

Intelligence And Temperament Of The Basset Bleu De Gascogne

You probably have a fair notion of how this dog behaves if you've ever met a hound.

This dog is really friendly toward almost everyone. Unlike other dogs, they do not greet you with excessive vigor. Instead, they are usually peaceful and relaxed.

They are far more trainable than the majority of hounds out there since they are quite simple to please. When they are younger, they may also be a little bit playful.

However, as kids age, this playfulness frequently decreases. When not out hunting, adult Basset Bleu De Gascognes spend a lot of time lounging about.

Unexpectedly, these dogs are remarkably resilient. They may trot for what seems like ages. Despite this, they do not have high exercise requirements or are hyperactive. They behave nicely indoors and don't leap too much.

Being a scent hound, the Basset Bleu De Gascogne should be kept indoors or on a leash while going outside.

They tend to get lost because they will take just about any track they come across.

They focus solely on hunting during hunting, so they lose track of time and are unable to figure out how to return.

This dog is not particularly intellectual, but it does become bored rapidly. They shouldn't be left alone for extended periods of time because of this. The best toys for these dogs are puzzles, but some of them aren't food-driven enough to play with them. Training and walks are excellent for occupying them, especially if you let them to sniff things.

This dog barks a lot, as you would expect from a hound. We do not advise them for flats because of this. They have a tendency to be highly talkative and can bay loudly.

CHAPTER FOUR

What Every Owner Of A Basset Bleu De Gascogne Should Know

Training

Typically, this dog is very eager to please. But they may also be obstinate at times. Like most dog breeds, the Basset Bleu De Gascogne frequently has a "teenager" phase between the ages of 1-2.

They could act more obstinate than normal at this point. Even if they don't seem to be paying attention, you must continue instructing them.

When they are fully mature, all the commands could appear to "click" at once.

When handled properly, they typically adapt to instruction quickly. Since they might be a little sensitive, gentle approaches are recommended.

Personality

A lively breed, the Basset Bleu de Gascogne is a wonderful addition to an active household. Although they don't have a reputation for being violent, they will hunt for smaller animals both outside and inside. Similar to Bassett Hounds, they enjoy singing and are typically vocal puppies. This breed is better suited for living in a house rather than an apartment because your neighbors might not like their singing.

A fragrance can quickly draw these dogs away. They are therefore challenging to train. If they scent anything fascinating, commands just fall on deaf ears. A novice dog owner should not get a Basset Bleu de Gascogne.

To train, they need experience, effort, and time. They make up for their short attention span with tenderness, though. These puppies adore their owners and lavish them with attention.

Size

The medium-sized Basset Bleu de Gascogne dog's length more than makes up for their height. They are just around a foot tall and weigh 35 to 40 pounds on average. In this regard, they resemble the Bassett Hound greatly, but their skin is far less floppy. They weigh roughly ten pounds less than their cousin breed due of their tight skin.

CHAPTER FIVE

Care

The Basset Bleu de Gascogne needs a good deal of physical activity. They should have at least two hours of daily walking time, as well as free time to play in between walks. It is advised that you incorporate games that require thought because these puppies enjoy to utilize their brains. This breed needs plenty of exercise in addition to lots of affection.

This dog would probably want to snuggle after taking a stroll to let off some steam. For this breed, physical love is equally as crucial as exercise.

Because they enjoy lounging, the Basset Bleu de Gascogne might not be the best choice if you don't want to let your dog join you on the couch.

Feeding

The food of a medium-sized, high-energy dog should be offered to Basset Bleu de Gascogne puppies. This breed's skin is also naturally oily, thus a diet rich in vitamin A may aid to reduce oiliness.

It's advisable to see your veterinarian to find out the finest food to feed your dog because every dog has different dietary needs.

Exercise

There is no strenuous workout required for the Basset Bleu De Gascogne. They are unhurried dogs. All they require to be content and healthy is one quick to medium-length stroll every day. A fenced-in backyard is usually a nice alternative for outside fun.

When left alone, these dogs frequently became couch potatoes. It is crucial that you motivate kids to exercise because of this. Either bring out the toys or take them on their regular stroll.

They are prone to obesity because of their relaxed outlook on life. As their back and joints are already sensitive, this might result in major issues. This breed must be kept as thin as possible, which typically implies that frequent activity is crucial.

CHAPTER SIX

Medical Conditions

In general, these canines are in good shape. They are nonetheless predisposed to a few health issues that need further discussion because they are preventable.

Obesity

These dogs might be a little sluggish. They are more likely to become obese as a result. Due to the added weight's impact on their system, this may result in cardiac and bone issues. They must maintain a healthy weight in order to avoid developing other issues.

Additionally, it's crucial to have regular vet appointments. When you see your dog every day, it may occasionally be challenging to determine whether or not they are overweight.

Skin Diseases

It is common for the Basset Bleu De Gascogne to have skin irritations and infections. In general, chemical items should be avoided and soft soap should be used to bathe them.

They should consume high-quality meals because lower-quality selections might result in skin issues.

Visit your veterinarian as soon as you discover any skin issues to rule out infections and receive treatment.

The dangerous disorder known as intervertebral disc disease (IVDD) can cause paralysis. Because of their longer back than other dogs', they have spinal column issues. Over a longer period of time, their back must bear all of their weight. Their spinal bones may degenerate as a result, which may lead to burst and herniated discs.

This might cause the dog major issues. A sudden injury, such something falling on the dog's back, might also result in IVDD.

Pain and a lack of coordination in the rear legs are the typical symptoms. When handled, the dog could scream and remain still. This illness often advances swiftly. The dog's rear legs can stop sensation in a matter of hours or days. Weakness and eventually paralysis may result from this. Without medical care, the dog won't be able to regulate their bladder or move their legs.

Fortunately, getting well is easy. Most dogs respond well to enforced crate rest within a few days, and most return to their former selves within a week or two. Inactivity reduces irritability and helps the back's swelling to go down.

Anti-inflammatory drugs may occasionally be given to the dog to further reduce the swelling, particularly if cage rest isn't having the desired effect.

Surgery is an option, although results might vary. The dog is at danger of anesthesia and it doesn't always work. It is frequently the last option because of this.

CHAPTER SEVEN

Coat Care And Color

The short, velvety coat of the Basset Bleu de Gascogne has to be brushed once a week. They shed a lot, like most shorthaired dogs do. Shedding is reduced by brushing.

These canines have a speckled look and are black and white. They often have tan patterns on their paws, snout, and neck.

Their coat might be oily, so to prevent odor, they may need to take semi-regular baths using an anti-fungal shampoo.

Ear cleaning is a crucial part of caring for the Basset Bleu de Gascogne. These puppies' large ears require care to prevent ear infections brought on by wax accumulation.

Ask your veterinarian for advice on the best wax buildup cleansing products to ensure your dog receives the best care possible.

Remember to take your dog to the vet for regular nail trims, as you should with all dogs. These canines have strong, black nails that have a propensity to grow fast, just like Bassett Hounds.

For families with older children, the Basset Bleu de Gascogne is a wise choice. Although they are known to get along well with kids of all ages, their high levels of activity might accidentally hurt younger kids. This breed gets along well with both cats and other dogs.

The Basset Bleu de Gascogne should not, however, be left unattended with rats or other small animals. They see these species as prey since they are hunting dogs.

To maintain a secure atmosphere for everyone, dogs must always be appropriately introduced to kids and other animals in the home.

Final Reflections

A uncommon breed of Basset hound that resembles other Basset hounds is the Basset Bleu De Gascogne. Their most distinctive feature among Basset hound breeds is their blue ticking physique, which is their claim to fame.

They are excellent for a wide range of families, whether or not they have kids, due to their laid-back attitude.

They don't need much activity, but it's crucial that they do in order to prevent illnesses like IVDD.

The primary issue with adopting these dogs is how hard it is to locate them. Outside of France, they are nearly unheard of, however there are a handful in the UK. Other things you might be interested in include: Grand Bleu De Gascogne and Gascon Saintongeois.

THE END

Printed in Great Britain
by Amazon